ACOUSTIC GUITAR MAGAZINE'S PRIVATE LESSONS

THE ACOUSTIC GUITAR METHOD

T0078728

BY DAVID HAMBURGER

BOOK 2

 STRING LETTER

Publisher: David A. Lusterman
Editor: Jeffrey Pepper Rodgers
Editorial Director: Simone Solondz
Music Editor and Engraver: Andrew DuBrock
Design and Production: Michael Zipkin, Lucid Design
Cover Design: Trpti Todd
Production Director: Ellen Richman
Marketing: Jen Fujimoto

Cover photograph: Rory Earnshaw
Photographs: pages 15, 17, 32, 36, Barbara Gelfand; page 46, Todd Wolfson.

Contents © 2001 David Hamburger
ISBN 1-890490-49-O

**STRING
LETTER**

CONTENTS

The complete set of audio tracks for the musical examples and songs in *The Acoustic Guitar Method, Book Two* is available for free download at AcousticGuitar.com/AGM2Audio. Just add the tracks to your shopping cart and enter the discount code "AGM2TRACKS12" during checkout to activate your free download.

TRACK
CD

Page No.

WELCOME

Introduction TRACK **1**

Tune-Up TRACK **2**

Greetings, guitarist. Yes, as an esteemed graduate of Book 1, you are a guitarist now, playing real music: you know a variety of open chords and strums, some single-note melodies, and almost a dozen songs. Check out the summary of Book 1 below, pat yourself on the back for learning all that stuff already (see the Music Notation Key if you need a little refresher on how to read the music), and then get ready to dig in deeper.

In Book 2, you'll learn how to alternate the bass notes in a country backup pattern, how to connect chords with some classic bass runs, and how to play your first fingerpicking patterns. As you learn to play more tunes, you'll find out what makes a major scale work and what blue notes do to a melody, all while learning more notes on the fingerboard. And, of course, along the way you'll be learning to play more great songs from the American roots repertoire.

WHAT WE LEARNED IN BOOK 1

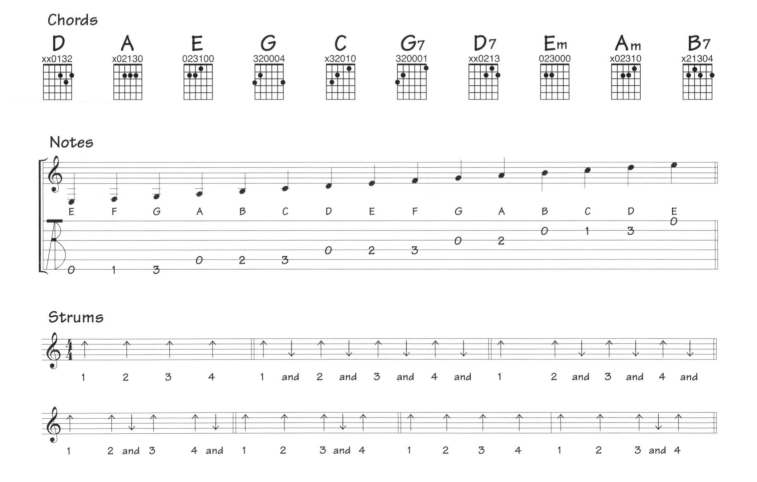

Need help with the lesson material in this book? Ask a question in our free, on-line support forum in the Guitar Talk section of www.acousticguitar.com.

MUSIC NOTATION KEY

The music in this book is written in standard notation and tablature. Here's how to read it.

Standard notation is written on a five-line staff. Notes are written in alphabetical order from A to G.

The duration of a note is determined by the note head, stem, and flag. A whole note (o) equals four beats. A half note (♩) is half of that: two beats. A quarter note (♩) equals one beat, and an eighth note (♪) equals half of one beat.

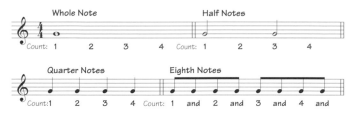

Rests indicate places where you don't play. A whole-note rest (⁻) lasts for four beats, a half-note rest (⁻) lasts for two beats, a quarter-note rest (𝄽) lasts for one beat, and an eighth-note rest (𝄾) lasts for half a beat.

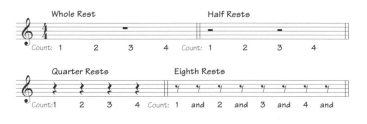

The fraction (4/4, 3/4, 6/8, etc.) shown at the beginning of a piece of music denotes the time signature or rhythmic pulse of the music. The top number tells you how many beats are in each measure, and the bottom number indicates the rhythmic value of each beat (4 equals a quarter note, 8 equals an eighth note, and 2 equals a half note). The most common time signature is 4/4, which signifies four quarter notes per measure. Waltz time, 3/4, has three quarter notes per measure.

Repeat symbols are placed at the beginning and end of the passage to be repeated.

You should ignore repeat symbols with the dots on the right side the first time you encounter them; when you come to a repeat symbol with dots on the left side, jump back to the

previous repeat symbol facing the opposite direction (if there is no previous symbol, go to the beginning of the piece). The next time you come to the repeat symbol, ignore it and keep going unless it includes instructions such as "Repeat three times."

In tablature, the six horizontal lines represent the six strings of the guitar, with the first string on the top and sixth on the bottom. The numbers tell you which fret to play on the given string. Tablature does not indicate rhythm values for the notes, so refer to the notation to know how long to play each note.

Chord diagrams show where the fingers go on the fingerboard. Frets are shown horizontally, and the thick top line represents the nut. The sixth (lowest-pitched) string is on the far left, and first (highest-pitched) string is on the far right. Dots show where the fingers go, and the numbers above the diagram tell you which fretting-hand fingers to use: 1 for the index finger, 2 the middle, 3 the ring, 4 the pinky, and *T* the thumb. An *X* indicates a string that should be muted or not played; 0 indicates an open string.

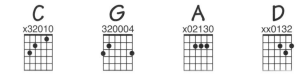

In strumming patterns, pick direction is shown with arrows: downstrokes are toward the floor, upstrokes toward the ceiling.

It might seem strange that an arrow pointing up indicates a downstroke and an arrow pointing down indicates an upstroke. Strums are written this way to be consistent with the notation and tablature, in which the lowest-pitched notes are at the bottom and highest-pitched notes are on top.

For single notes played with a pick, these symbols are used for downstrokes and upstrokes:

⊓ = downstroke   ∨ = upstroke

LESSON 1
THE ALTERNATING BASS

In Book 1, we played country backup parts by hitting a bass note on the first beat and following up with three downstroke strums (or two downstroke strums for a waltz). Now we're going to add in another bass note, on the third beat, replacing one of the strums and giving us the classic country and blue-grass sound of an *alternating bass.*

Let's start with a familiar chord, D. For now, our general rule is: for the sec-ond bass note of the pattern, go up to the next highest string (meaning the string with the next highest *pitch,* not the one higher off the floor). So for a D chord, we'll play the second fret, third string, on beat 3, as in Example 1. Everything is still done with all downstrokes (toward the floor).

On an A chord, if we follow the general rule of going up to the next highest string for the bass note, we'll play an E note, or the second fret on the fourth string, on beat 3. It will sound like Example 2. You're now playing a bass note on every other beat, and following every bass note with a downward strum on the top strings.

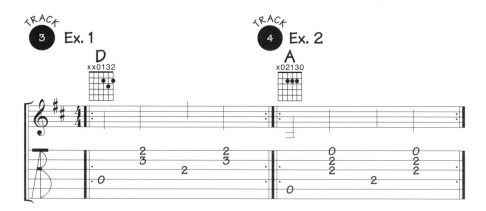

As you might have guessed, the interesting part is keeping this going as you switch chords. To get used to maintaining an alternating-bass strum for each chord, practice switching between D and A every two bars, as in Example 3.

If you're having trouble hitting the right strings for the bass notes, take out the strums for a moment. Just try socking away at the first and third beats of the D chord, as in Example 4, paying attention to hitting each string as accu-rately as possible. You should still finger the whole chord while you do this exercise. In Example 5, do the same thing with the A chord: just play the bass notes.

When you go back to playing the whole strum, continue to focus on hitting the bass notes on beats 1 and 3, and let the strums fall almost as an afterthought.

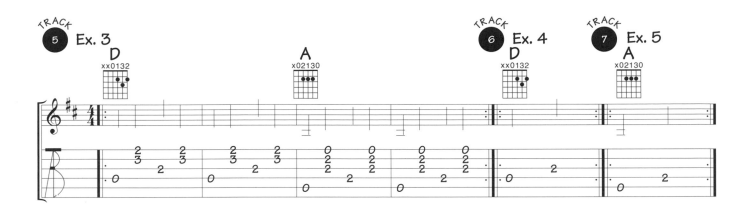

ALTERNATING BASS ON G

Let's move on to another chord. To play an alternating-bass strum on G, we're going to break our general rule about the second bass note: we're going to go up two strings, to the open fourth string, for our bass note on beat 3. It will sound like Example 6. Again, to troubleshoot: if that skip from the sixth to the fourth string is hanging you up, take out the strums and just play the bass notes, as in Example 7.

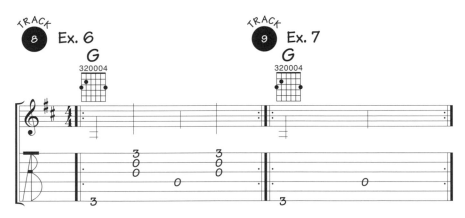

Let's make sure we can connect G to both D and A using alternating-bass strum patterns. First, try G to A and back in Example 8. From G to D involves a bit of a wrinkle: the upper bass note you play on beat 3 of a G chord, a D on the open fourth string, is the same note as you play on the first beat of the D chord. It may feel a little odd that in terms of bass notes, your picking hand is staying in the same place while your fretting hand is changing chords. But it sounds good: try it in Example 9.

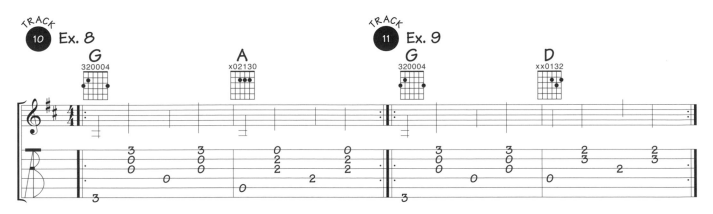

THE COMPLETE "COLUMBUS"

Let's play something with all three chords now. In Book 1, we played the *verse* to "Columbus Stockade Blues"; the *chorus* (the section that repeats, also known as the *refrain*) involves going to a G chord. Notice that the second half of the chorus uses the same chord progression as the verse we already know.

First try the chorus by itself, then put the whole song together: verse and chorus, all with alternating-bass strumming. Bring on the parking-lot jam session!

COLUMBUS STOCKADE BLUES

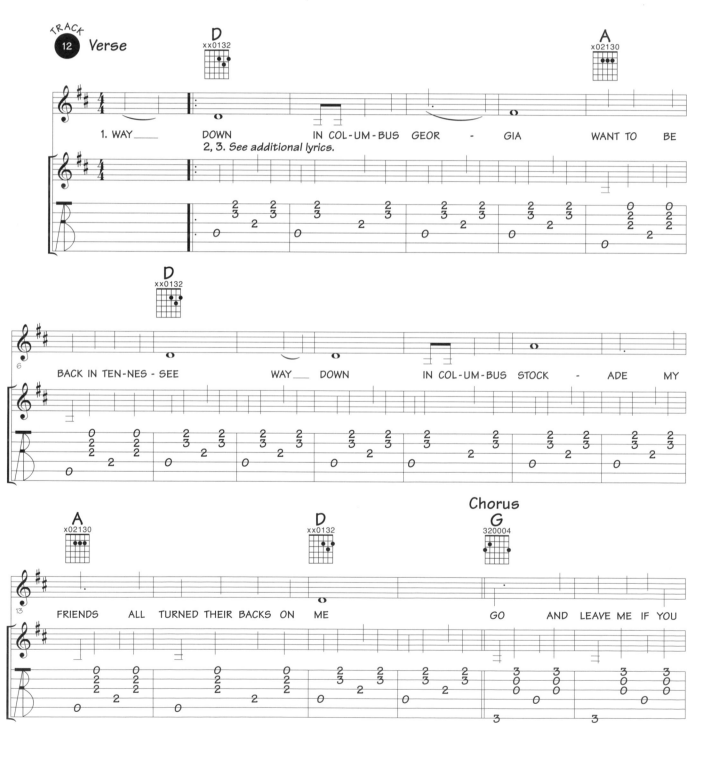

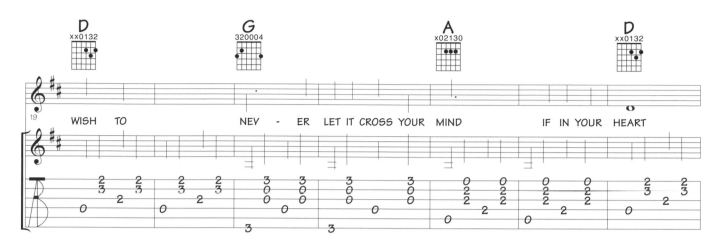

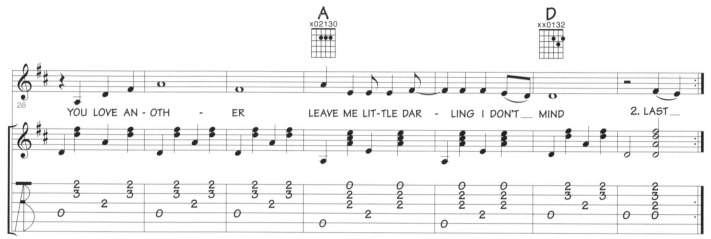

	D
1.	WAY DOWN IN COLUMBUS, GEORGIA,

1.
    D
WAY DOWN IN COLUMBUS, GEORGIA,
A   **D**
WANT TO BE BACK IN TENNESSEE

WAY DOWN IN COLUMBUS STOCKADE
  A   **D**
MY FRIENDS ALL TURNED THEIR BACKS ON ME

  G   **D**
GO AND LEAVE ME IF YOU WISH TO
  G   **A**
NEVER LET IT CROSS YOUR MIND
       D
IF IN YOUR HEART YOU LOVE ANOTHER
A   **D**
LEAVE ME LITTLE DARLING I DON'T MIND

2.
        D
LAST NIGHT AS I LAY SLEEPING
  A   **D**
I DREAMT I HELD YOU IN MY ARMS

WHEN I AWOKE I WAS MISTAKEN
A   **D**
I WAS PEERING THROUGH THE BARS

   CHORUS

3.
       D
MANY A NIGHT WITH YOU I RAMBLED
A   **D**
MANY AN HOUR WITH YOU I SPENT

THOUGHT I HAD YOUR HEART FOREVER
   A   **D**
NOW I FIND IT WAS ONLY LENT

   CHORUS

LESSON 2
BLUES IN E

Let's add two more chords to our alternating-bass stash. For E, we'll follow our original rule: the first bass note is on the sixth string, and the second bass note is one string up, on the fifth string. That second note will be a B, at the second fret of the fifth string, on beat 3 (Example 1).

For B7, with its root on the fifth string, we'll also go up one string for the second bass note. On B7, that turns out to be a D♯, or the first fret on the fourth string (Example 2). A sharp symbol (♯) raises a note by a half step, or one fret. So a D♯ is one fret above the D note on the fourth string.

In Example 3, let's try making the move from E to A and back again with just

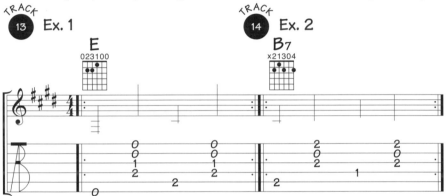

one measure per chord, using an alternating-bass strum pattern. If this is moving too quickly for you, just back off and play two measures of each chord at first. Then, try two measures of one chord and one measure of the other, as in Example 4, where you play two measures of A followed by one measure of E and then repeat it.

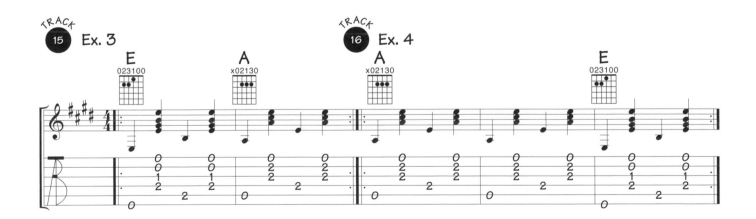

Now try the move from E to B7. Your right hand is doing the exact same moves as it did to switch from E to A: from bass notes on the sixth and fifth strings to bass notes on the fifth and fourth strings.

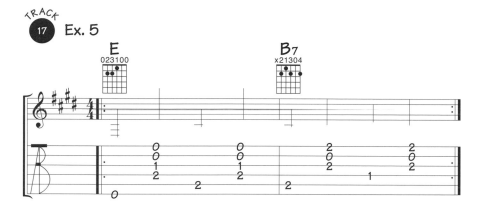

A CLASSIC BLUES

On to our next tune. With E, A, and B7 we're equipped to play the classic blues story-song "Stagolee." Note the quick switch from one bar of E up to B7 in measures 8–9. If it gives you any trouble, go back and spend a little more time with Example 5, which isolates that change.

ESSENTIAL LISTENING

Like "Careless Love," which we played in Book 1, **"Stagolee"** (also known as "Stack o' Lee Blues," "Stagger Lee," "Stackerlee," "Stack Lee" . . .) is one of those tunes that has appealed to jazz musicians as well as to blues singers. Sol Hoopii was a Hawaiian steel guitarist who played slide solos in a hot jazz style and influenced the role of the Dobro in bluegrass and country; he plays "Stack o' Lee" on *Master of the Hawaiian Guitar,* Vol. 1 (Rounder). Also check out Ma Rainey's early jazz version on *Ma Rainey's Black Bottom* (Yazoo). For the folk and blues side of things, try **Mississippi John Hurt**'s *1928 Sessions* (Yazoo), Woody Guthrie's *Muleskinner Blues: The Asch Recordings,* Vol. 2 (Smithsonian Folkways), or Tim and Mollie O'Brien's *Remember Me* (Sugar Hill).

STAGOLEE

1. STAG-O-LEE_ WAS A BAD MAN   EV-'RY-BO-DY KNOWS_   SPENT A HUN-DRED DOL-LARS JUST TO
2–6. See additional lyrics.

BUY HIM A SUIT OF CLOTHES ____   HE'S A BAD ____ MAN   CRUEL ____ STAG-O-LEE ____

    E
1. STAGOLEE WAS A BAD MAN, EV'RYBODY KNOWS
  A   E
SPENT A HUNDRED DOLLARS JUST TO BUY HIM A SUIT OF CLOTHES
      B7   E
HE'S A BAD MAN, CRUEL STAGOLEE

    E
2. STAGOLEE SHOT BILLY DE LYONS, WHAT DO YOU THINK ABOUT THAT
  A   E
SHOT HIM DOWN IN COLD BLOOD, 'CAUSE HE STOLE HIS STETSON HAT
      B7   E
HE'S A BAD MAN, THAT CRUEL STAGOLEE

    E
3. BILLY DE LYONS SAID, "STAGOLEE, PLEASE DON'T TAKE MY LIFE
      A   E
I GOT TWO LITTLE BABIES AND A DARLIN' LOVIN' WIFE"
      B7   E
THAT BAD MAN, OH, CRUEL STAGOLEE

    E
4. "WHAT I CARE ABOUT YOUR TWO LITTLE BABIES, YOUR

      DARLIN' LOVIN' WIFE?
      A   E
YOU DONE STOLE MY STETSON HAT, I'M BOUND TO TAKE YOUR LIFE"
      B7   E
HE'S A BAD MAN, CRUEL STAGOLEE

    E
5. GENTLEMEN OF THE JURY, WHAT DO YOU THINK OF THAT?
  A   E
STAGOLEE KILLED BILLY DE LYON FOR A FIVE-DOLLAR STETSON HAT
      B7   E
HE'S A BAD MAN, CRUEL STAGOLEE

    E
6. EVERYBODY GATHERED, HANDS WAY UP HIGH
      A
AT TWELVE O'CLOCK THEY KILLED HIM, THEY WERE GLAD TO
        E
SEE HIM DIE
      B7   E
THAT BAD MAN, CRUEL STAGOLEE

LESSON 3
MAJOR SCALES AND MELODIES

In Book I we learned a handful of melodies; now we're going to look at the *scales* that they're based on. A scale is a specific collection of notes, and you can think of them as containing the building blocks of melodies, much the way chords are the building blocks of a song's structure or chord progression. Let's learn a little bit about scales and then hear one at work in a traditional melody.

Like chords, scales can be major or minor (or have other qualities) and, also like chords, there's a scale for every letter in the musical alphabet. So there's a C-major scale, a D-major scale, an E-major scale, and so on, just as there is a C chord, a D chord, an E chord, and all the other ones you know. What does a scale sound like? Well, here's a C-major scale, which will probably sound pretty familiar:

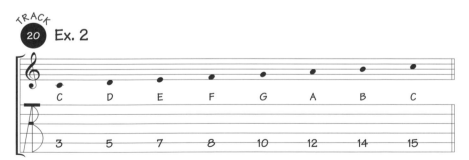

Notice that there's one note of every letter in the scale. It's a C scale because it starts and ends on C, but what makes it major? That has to do with the spaces between the notes. Take the same scale and play it all on one string, the fifth string.

If you remember our discussion about half steps and whole steps in Book I, you can count which notes here are a whole step (two frets) apart and which notes are just a half step (one fret) apart. We get this pattern as we go up the scale: whole step, whole step, half step, whole step, whole step, whole step, half step. This is often abbreviated: W W H W W W H.

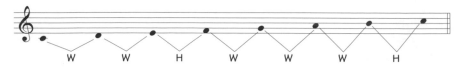

ESSENTIAL LISTENING

Back in Book 1, we played "Ida Red" and talked
a little bit about Bob Wills and the Texas
Playboys, the kings of western swing. **"The Girl
I Left Behind Me"** was also in Wills' repertoire
and can be heard on *The Tiffany Transcriptions,*
Vol. 1 (Rhino). Also check out multi-instrumen-
talist Erik Darling's performance on *Instrumental
Music and Songs of the Southern Appalachians*
(Tradition), and for a bluegrass take, try Blue
Highway's *It's a Long, Long Road* (Rebel).

We've already seen how you can play one note in more than one *register;* for
example, we know how to play the note A on the open fifth string as well as at
the second fret of the third string. Likewise, we've played G both at the third fret
of the sixth string and at the open third string. Example 1 spells out a C scale in
one octave, which runs from one C note to the next highest one. You could also
play any of these notes, and this same scale, in another register—higher up the
guitar neck. A melody that sticks to just these seven notes, whatever octave
they are played in, is said to be in the key of C.

Here's a tune that illustrates this idea. "The Girl I Left Behind Me" is another
traditional melody that lies well on the guitar, and in this arrangement all the
notes are from the C-major scale. It includes two notes we mentioned, the A and
G that are below the lowest C on the fretboard, as well as the low B (which we've
learned as the bass note of a B7 chord). These notes are still in the C scale even
though they're in a lower register than the one-octave version of the scale we
know. Otherwise, all the notes lie within the one-octave scale of Example 1.

Alternate downstrokes and upstrokes for the eighth notes, as written; otherwise just use downstrokes.

THE GIRL I LEFT BEHIND ME

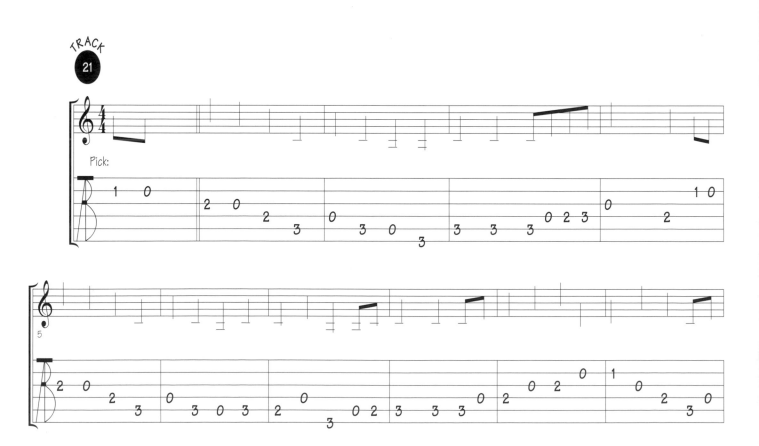

LESSON 4
STARTING TO FINGERPICK

So far we've been strumming and playing single notes with a pick (aka *flatpicking*), rather than our fingers. It's time to introduce *fingerstyle* or *fingerpicking* technique, which means that you literally pick the strings with your individual fingers and your thumb rather than with a pick. The great country blues, ragtime, and gospel guitarists were nearly all fingerpickers, with stylists like Mississippi John Hurt and Reverend Gary Davis exerting an enormous influence over subsequent generations of musicians. While flatpicking rules the bluegrass roost, there are exceptions (Lester Flatt, for one); meanwhile, two of the most influential fingerstylists come from the country tradition: Merle Travis and Chet Atkins.

We'll start by assigning the thumb and fingers to particular strings and use this idea to learn some basic *patterns*. Just as we learned to play one kind of strum pattern on several chords, we'll now take one way of fingerpicking the notes of a chord and learn how to switch between the various chords of a song while keeping the same pattern going. This idea is called (would you have guessed?) *pattern picking*.

GETTING IN POSITION

Let's start with a D chord. For our first pattern, we're going to use the index, middle, and ring fingers along with the thumb. Here's how these fingers are indicated in the notation:

p = thumb i = index m = middle a = ring

"Dave," I hear you say, "come on. *Thumb* starts with a *t*, not a *p*. And *ring* starts with an *r*, not an *a*. What's all this *p, i, m, a* stuff about?" Well, it comes from classical guitar notation, where *p* stands for *pulgar*, *i* stands for *indice*, *m* stands for *medio*, and *a* stands for *anular* (the Spanish words for thumb, index finger, middle finger, and ring finger). It takes a little getting used to, but this is how picking-hand fingerings are often indicated.

To start, rest your thumb on the fourth string, your index finger on the third string, your middle finger on the second string, and your ring finger on the first string.

Got that? Now, look at your fingers and thumb. You want to have your thumb about an inch closer to the fingerboard than your fingers, and your fingers should be somewhat curled up, without too big an arch to your wrist. If your fingers

Rest your thumb and fingers on the top four strings, then move your thumb closer to the fingerboard.

and thumb are all bunched together, try sliding your thumb along the strings toward the fingerboard as you slide your fingers back toward the bridge.

For now, your fingers are assigned to these strings: you're always going to use your thumb for the fourth string, index for the third, middle for the second string, and ring for the first string. To get used to this, lift your fingers from the strings as a group, then drop them back down onto the strings again. This is a lot like the exercise we did at the beginning of Book 1 to get used to landing your fingers together on a particular chord.

OK, now that you've gotten your fingers identified with the strings they're going to play, lift your hand up so your fingertips are hovering maybe half an inch above the strings. That's where you want to keep your hand when you play; if you leave your fingers resting on the strings, you'll keep those strings from ringing out.

FIRST PATTERN

On to the first pattern. You're going to just go up the strings, picking each string once, as in Example 1. Just think of it as rolling up the strings: thumb, index, middle, then ring. When that feels comfortable, try doing it two times in a row (Example 2).

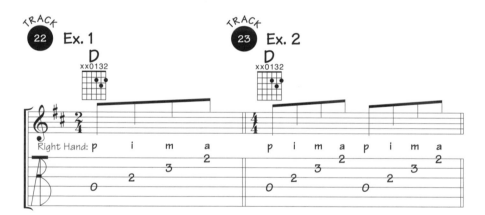

There it is: your first pattern. This is one of those things that basically just gets better with simple and constant repetition. Do it slowly enough to get every note sounding even and clear. Note: Unlike strumming, fingerpicking isolates every note of a chord, so it's kind of like a lie detector test for your left hand. You find out just how clearly—or not—you've been fretting your chords.

"Swell," I hear you say, "but Dave, how do I apply this pattern to, say, a C chord? Can I just change my left hand and let 'er rip?"

Well, almost. Keep your index, middle, and ring fingers on the same strings, but move your thumb down to the fifth string. Why? Well, this kind of pattern picking is like the first country backup bass/strum we did, in that you always want to pick out the root or bottom note of the chord on the first beat of the pattern. So, on a C chord, you could pick the fourth string with your thumb, because it's part of the chord, but the pattern will sound a lot fuller with a big fat C at the beginning. Like Example 3. To get used to repeating this pattern, try Example 4.

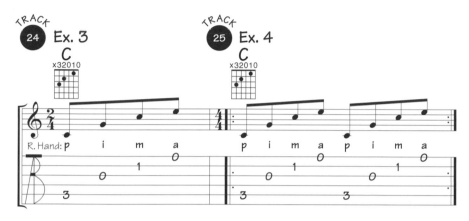

In Book I we learned the melody to "Shady Grove"; now let's play the chords using our first picking pattern. We'll need a new chord, too—D minor.

There's going to be a quick change between D minor and C in measure 7, where you have to play half a bar of the pattern on D minor and half a bar on C, then switch back to D minor again. To get used to that move, and to practice forming a D minor with your left hand, spend some time with these two exercises. In Example 5, play half a measure of D minor, then just the first note of the C pattern. In Example 6, play half a measure of D minor, half a measure of C, and then just the first note of the D pattern again.

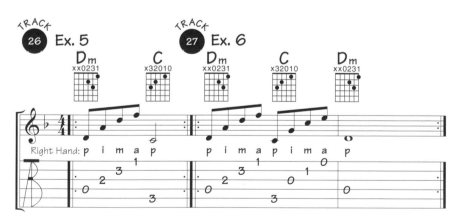

Now try the whole tune.

SHADY GROVE

Dm   C
SHADY GROVE MY LITTLE LOVE
Dm
SHADY GROVE I KNOW
         C
SHADY GROVE MY LITTLE LOVE
Dm   C   Dm
BOUND FOR SHADY GROVE

     Dm   C
1.   I WISH I HAD A BANJO STRING
     Dm
MADE OF GOLDEN TWINE
         C
EVERY TUNE I'D PICK ON IT
    Dm   C   Dm
I'D WISH THAT GIRL WAS MINE

       CHORUS

     Dm   C
2.   I WENT TO SEE MY SHADY GROVE
        Dm
SHE WAS STANDING IN THE DOOR
         C
SHOES AND STOCKINGS IN HER HAND
       Dm   C   Dm
AND HER LITTLE BARE FEET ON THE FLOOR

     Dm   C
3.   I WISH I HAD ME A BIG FINE HORSE
        Dm
AND THE CORN TO FEED HIM ON
            C
LITTLE SHADY GROVE TO STAY AT HOME
      Dm   C   Dm
AND FEED HIM WHILE I'M GONE

       CHORUS

     Dm   C
4.   PEACHES IN THE SUMMERTIME
     Dm
APPLES IN THE FALL
          C
IF I CAN'T GET THE GIRL I LOVE
     Dm   C   Dm
I DON'T WANT NONE AT ALL

     Dm   C
5.   NOW WHEN I WAS A LITTLE BOY
     Dm
I WANTED A BARLOW KNIFE
          C
AND NOW I WANT MY SHADY GROVE
     Dm   C   Dm
TO SAY SHE'LL BE MY WIFE

LESSON 5
MORE PICKING PATTERNS

Let's apply our first fingerpicking pattern to a G chord. To do so, keep playing the top three strings with your index, middle, and ring fingers, but move your thumb all the way down to the sixth string, so that when we start the pattern on a G chord we've got a big low G in the bass:

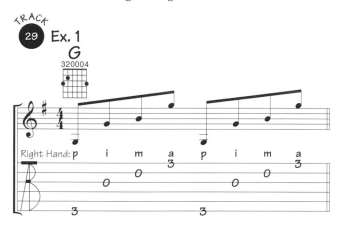

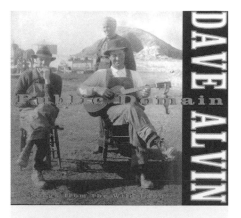

Now the trick is going to be moving from chord to chord, bringing your thumb along to the right bass string while keeping your picking fingers the same on top. In Example 2, try switching between G and C. In Example 3, try switching between G and D.

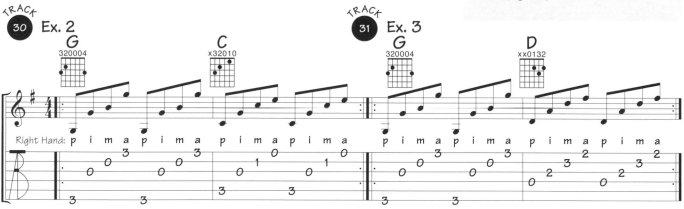

If your left hand is tripping you up as you try these new right-hand moves, leave the chords out for a moment: just practice making the right-hand pattern switches while playing the open strings. It will sound less than beautiful, per-haps, but it will let you focus on one thing at a time—in this case, bringing your thumb over to the right string. Then, when you feel like you're getting the hang of it, add the chords back in.

Let's use this picking pattern to play the lyrical old folk song "Shenandoah."

SHENANDOAH

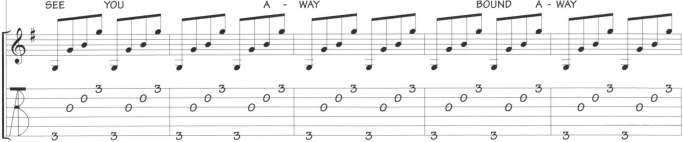

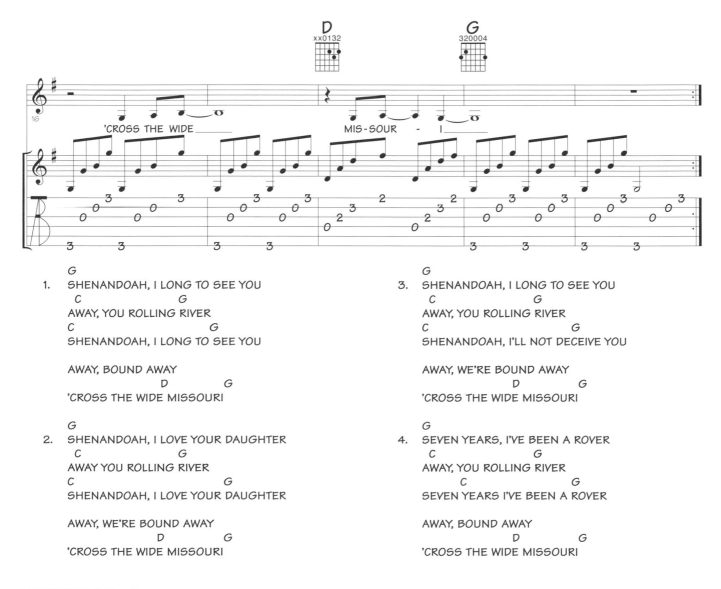

1. G
   SHENANDOAH, I LONG TO SEE YOU
      C   G
   AWAY, YOU ROLLING RIVER
   C   G
   SHENANDOAH, I LONG TO SEE YOU

   AWAY, BOUND AWAY
                D   G
   'CROSS THE WIDE MISSOURI

2. G
   SHENANDOAH, I LOVE YOUR DAUGHTER
      C   G
   AWAY YOU ROLLING RIVER
   C   G
   SHENANDOAH, I LOVE YOUR DAUGHTER

   AWAY, WE'RE BOUND AWAY
                D   G
   'CROSS THE WIDE MISSOURI

3. G
   SHENANDOAH, I LONG TO SEE YOU
      C   G
   AWAY, YOU ROLLING RIVER
   C   G
   SHENANDOAH, I'LL NOT DECEIVE YOU

   AWAY, WE'RE BOUND AWAY
                D   G
   'CROSS THE WIDE MISSOURI

4. G
   SEVEN YEARS, I'VE BEEN A ROVER
      C   G
   AWAY, YOU ROLLING RIVER
          C   G
   SEVEN YEARS I'VE BEEN A ROVER

   AWAY, BOUND AWAY
                D   G
   'CROSS THE WIDE MISSOURI

PATTERN NO. 2

Let's move on to another pattern. For this one, your middle and ring fingers are going to operate as a pair, picking the second and first strings simultaneously. In Example 4, try just that first, while fretting a D chord.

In Example 5, try rolling up the strings of a D chord by playing the thumb on the fourth string and then the index finger on the third string, followed by the second and first strings played together. And in Example 6, come back to the third string with your index finger after playing the top two strings together.

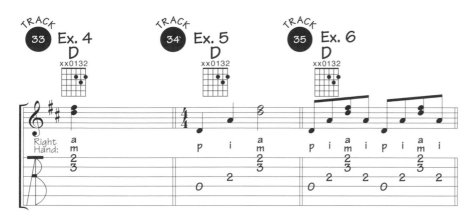

To move this pattern to an A chord, start your thumb on the fifth string while keeping your index, middle, and ring fingers on the top three strings, as in Example 7. For a G chord, keep your fingers in the same place while you bring your thumb down to the sixth string:

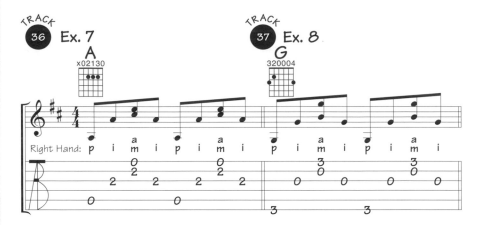

Example 7 includes a new note: C♯, at the second fret of the second string. We've actually been playing this note all along as part of an A chord but this is the first time we've had to read it. Remember the idea behind sharps: C♯ is the note you get when you raise a C one fret, or a half step. At the beginning Example 7, there's a ♯ symbol on the C and F spaces; this means that all C and F notes that follow are sharp. We'll talk more about this kind of notation when we continue our discussion of scales in the next lesson.

"CIRCLE" TIME

Practice these moves on the tune "Will the Circle Be Unbroken?"

WILL THE CIRCLE BE UNBROKEN?

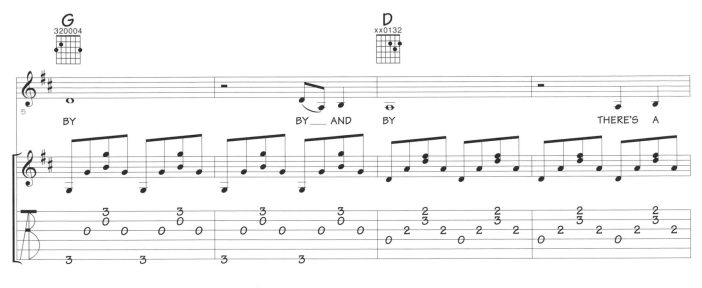

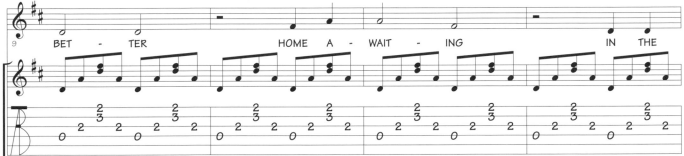

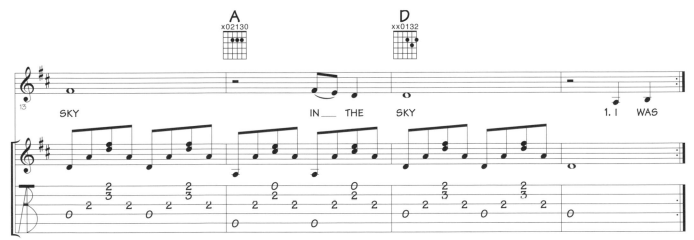

D
WILL THE CIRCLE BE UNBROKEN
        G   D
BY AND BY, BY AND BY

THERE'S A BETTER HOME A-WAITING
          A   D
IN THE SKY, IN THE SKY

            D
1. I WAS STANDING BY THE WINDOW
        G   D
ON A COLD AND RAINY DAY

WHEN I SAW THAT HEARSE COME ROLLING
                A   D
FOR TO TAKE MY MOTHER AWAY

    CHORUS

                        D
2. WELL I TOLD THE UNDERTAKER
        G   D
UNDERTAKER, PLEASE DRIVE SLOW

FOR THAT BODY YOU'RE A-CARRYING
                A   D
WELL I HATE TO SEE IT GO

    CHORUS

LESSON 6
THE G-MAJOR SCALE

And now, dig through your pockets or between the cushions of the couch for one of those little plastic triangles, because we're going to resume playing with a pick in this lesson. In Lesson 3, we talked about the fact that there's a formula for the major scale: you start and end on the same note, play one of every note in between, and always have the same combination of half steps and whole steps between notes. Before we go ahead and try making a G-major scale, we'll need to learn a couple more notes on the fingerboard: F and G on the first string.

We were introduced to the E on the first string back when we learned the six open strings of the guitar; it's shown on the top space of the staff. F is always a half step or one fret up from E, so in this case it's found at the first fret of the first string and shown on the top line of the staff. G is a whole step or two frets up from F, so it's played at the third fret on the first string and shown just above the top line of the staff.

Now let's play one of every note from G on the third string to a G on the first string and see if it sounds like a G scale:

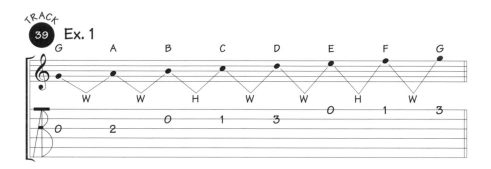

If you sing the familiar "do re mi fa sol la ti do" to this scale, you may notice that it sounds a little off toward the end. Let's count the half steps and whole steps and see if they fit our formula of W W H W W W H. From G to A is two frets, or a whole step; from A to B is also two frets, another whole step. B to C on the second string is a half step, then C to D and D to E are also whole steps. So far, so good. But now, E to F is a half step, where, according to the formula, we should have a half step. And then to end things, F to G is two frets, or a whole step, and that doesn't fit either.

What's the story? To make this a normal major scale, we need a way to create the correct order of whole and half steps. Raising the seventh note, F, a half step, makes the pattern fall into place. The name for an F note raised a half step is F sharp (F♯), and it's shown on the staff by putting a ♯ symbol in front of the F note itself. F♯ is a half step higher than F, so it's played at the second fret of the first string.

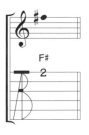

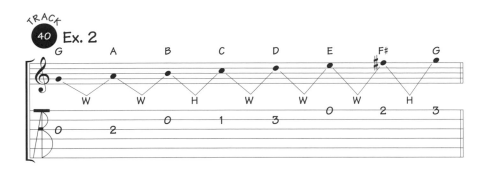

Using this F# in place of F, we've got the right arrangement of whole steps and half steps in our G-major scale. And if you listen to the scale with the F#, you'll hear that it has that "do re mi" scale sound all the way up to the top.

Here's a tune in the key of G that makes use of all the notes of this G-major scale. Note that we use a # symbol at the beginning of each staff. This tells you to play every F note that follows as an F#. Since doing so will create a melody in the key of G, this notation is called a *key signature*. There is a different key signature for every key.

The accompaniment part uses this pattern:

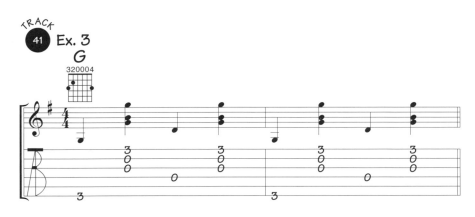

ESSENTIAL LISTENING

The **Holy Modal Rounders** are a perfect example of how you can get away with all kinds weirdness if you have the knowledge and the chops to back it up. The duo of fiddler Peter Stampfel and guitarist Steve Weber coalesced in the Greenwich Village folk scene in the early '60s, and while they clearly knew their old-time music, they didn't hold it sacred. Made-up verses and a careening, almost out-of-control performance style were par for the course, as was a repertoire that ranged from "Statesboro Blues" to "Clinch Mountain Backstep." Hear all that *and* their version of **"Sail Away Ladies"** on the Holy Modal Rounders' collection *1 & 2* (Fantasy).

The Rounders' setting of this tune borrows heavily from the classic version made popular by the first Grand Ole Opry star, Uncle Dave Macon. You can hear his rendering on *Go Long Mule* (County). On the *Anthology of American Folk Music* (Smithsonian Folkways) there's Uncle Bunt Stephens' unaccompanied version, recorded in 1926. The New Lost City Ramblers play "Ladies" on *Old Time Music* (Vanguard). Legendary Appalachian fiddler Tommy Jarrell does a wicked version on *The Legacy of Tommy Jarrell*, Vol 1: *Sail Away Ladies* (County).

SAIL AWAY LADIES

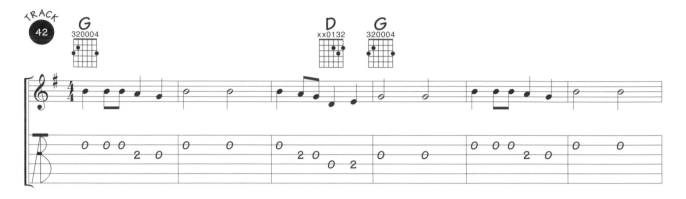

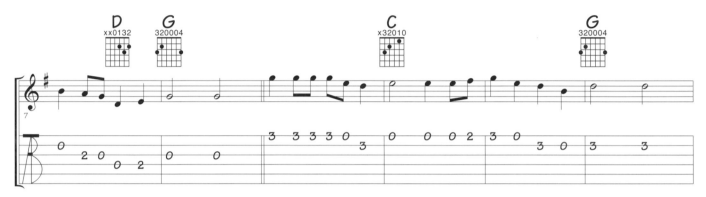

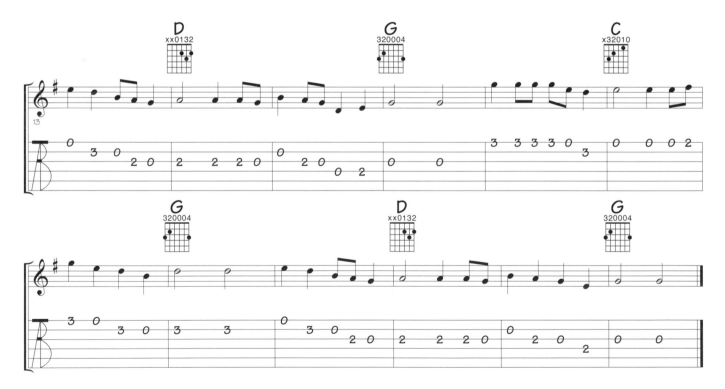

LESSON 7
BASS RUNS

We've already learned how to play a steady *boom-chick* bass/strum with an alternating bass; now it's time to add in some *bass runs*. A bass run is a short phrase, usually just two or three notes long, that helps to lead from one chord into another. For example, here's a bass run into G:

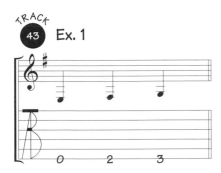

Before we get into how to use this run, notice that it introduces a new note, the low F♯ at the second fret on the sixth string. We've had F♯ on the first string already, and finding F♯ on the sixth string works the same way: it's a half step, or one fret, from E to F, so when you raise F a half step (one fret) to F♯, you're now a total of a whole step (two frets) up from E.

To play this bass run, you want to start so that when you land on the third note, G, it's actually the first bass note of our bass/strum pattern. So you count off as in Example 2. As you may remember from Book 1, this kind of phrase is called a *pickup*. Example 3 shows the bass run leading into two full measures of G.

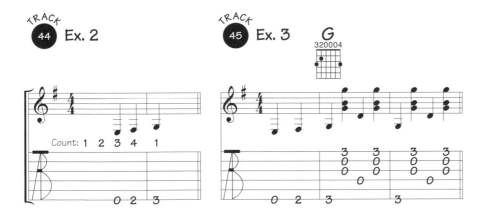

"OK," you're probably thinking, "that's cool, but what if I want to play this bass run again after a couple of measures of G?" Right. Well, all you've really got to do is take out the last two beats of the second full measure of G—one bass and one strum—and drop in the first two notes of the bass run, E and F♯.

Starting right on the downbeat, it will sound like Example 4. If you start with the bass-run pickup and just keep going in G, throwing the bass run in every two measures, it sounds like Example 5.

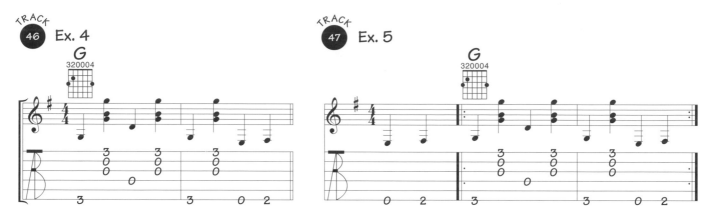

As they said in my high school French class, "Très cool, n'est pas?" Meaning, if I recall correctly, "Very cool, is it not?"

Now, since there are very few songs that have the consideration to just sit on a G chord the entire time, what we really want to do is use this bass run to get back to G from various other chords, like C and D for starters. So try Example 6: play two measures of alternating bass/strum on a D chord, but drop out the last bass/strum to play the bass run back up to G. Then in Example 7, add in a full two measures of G bass/strum.

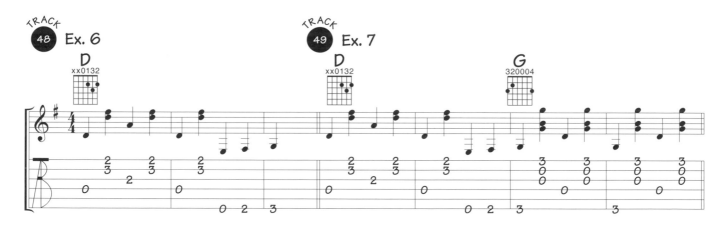

Before we go from a C chord to a G with the bass run, we'll need an alternating-bass pattern to play on a C chord. Start with the C on the fifth string, third fret, for the first bass note and go up to the fourth string, second fret (E), for the upper bass note.

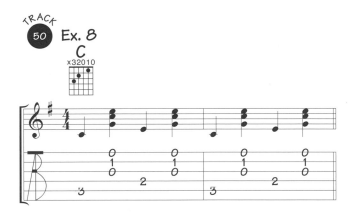

Next, just like we did on the D chord, take out the last bass/strum before going to the G, and drop in the bass run: E, F♯, G. Try it in Example 9. Then try going from C into the bass run and then playing two full measures of G with an alternating bass/strum (Example 10).

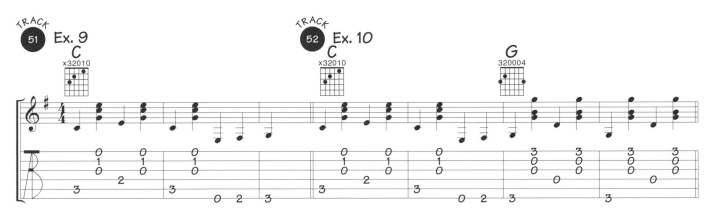

Let's put all this to use in "I Am a Pilgrim." The song is in the key of G, but you start on a D chord. Every time the G comes around, you get into it using the bass run, except in measure 14, where you've only got one measure of D before getting back to the G chord. Notice also that in measures 8–9, you play the bass run in the middle of a four-measure stretch of G, not unlike what we practiced in Example 5.

ESSENTIAL LISTENING

Merle Travis' *Folk Songs of the Hills* (Capitol), originally issued on a set of four 78-rpm records in 1947, featured the groundbreaking fingerstyle guitarist in a solo acoustic setting, doing traditional tunes and soon-to-be-standard originals like "Sixteen Tons" and "Dark as a Dungeon" as well as the expected folk material like **"I Am a Pilgrim."** Travis also pioneered the use of the electric guitar in country music, wrote western swing classics like "Smoke! Smoke! Smoke! That Cigarette" and clever wordplay tunes like "Divorce Me C.O.D.," and, with Paul Bigsby, helped develop a custom solid-body instrument that anticipated the design of Leo Fender's Telecaster. Speaking of which, check out the Byrds' version on their country-rock salvo *Sweetheart of the Rodeo* (Legacy); Byrds guitarist Clarence White can be heard playing the tune in another setting on *The Kentucky Colonels Featuring Clarence White* (Rounder).

I AM A PILGRIM

D   G
1.   I AM A PILGRIM AND A STRANGER
          C   G
     TRAV'LING THROUGH THIS WORRISOME LAND
                               C
     I'VE GOT A HOME IN THAT YONDER CITY
          G D   G
     AND IT'S NOT, NOT MADE BY HAND

D   G
2.   I'VE GOT A MOTHER, SISTER, AND BROTHER
          C   G
     WHO HAVE GONE, GONE ON BEFORE
                              C
     AND I'M DETERMINED TO GO AND MEET THEM
          G D   G
     OVER ON THAT OTHER SHORE

LESSON 8
MORE BASS RUNS

If you're thinking there must be a way to play a bass run into other chords besides G, you're right. The bass run into C looks a lot like the bass run in G moved up a string (which makes sense, considering how much the bottom notes of a C chord look like those of a G chord moved up one string). Here it is: the notes A, B, and C.

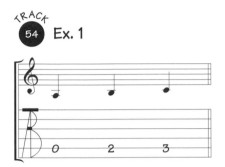

Like the G bass run, the C bass run starts two beats before the 1 of a bass/strum pattern. The third note of the C bass run, C, becomes the first bass note of a C bass/strum, as in Example 2.

If you want to just hang on a C chord, throwing in the bass run every other time, drop out the second bass/strum in the second measure of the pattern and replace it with the first two notes of the bass run, A and B (Example 3).

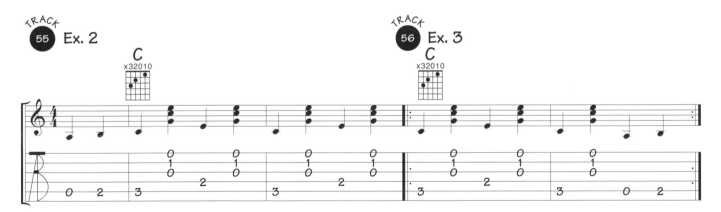

Try switching between C and G now, using a bass run every other measure to get into the next chord. In Example 4, you start on a pickup measure with a bass run up to a C chord, then halfway through measure 2 you play the G bass run into measure 3. At the end of measure 4, you play the C bass run up into the C chord, and keep going around like that.

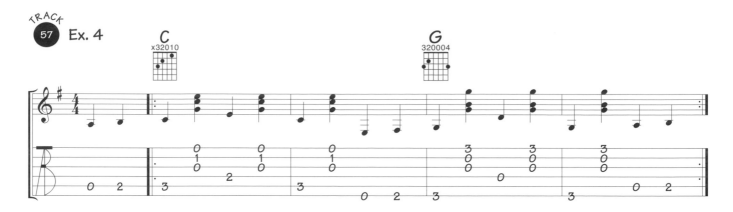

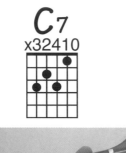

Let's add these moves into "I Am a Pilgrim." While we're at it, we'll add a couple of seventh chords to the arrangement as well. You already know G7, and we'll use it here to create more motion during the four bars of G in the middle of the tune, strengthening the transition up to C in the process. The C7 in measures 5–6 and 11–12 is a new chord. To play it, you put down your fingers for a regular C chord and then add in your pinky at the third fret of the third string.

This chord is a kind of optional sound—use it if you like it. You can hear a particularly tasteful use of the seventh-chord sound on David Grisman and Tony Rice's instrumental version of this tune, recorded on the first *Tone Poems* CD (Acoustic Disc). Here's "I Am a Pilgrim" with seventh chords added and bass runs into both G and C.

I AM A PILGRIM

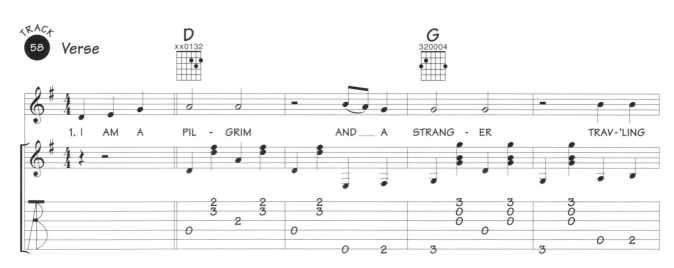

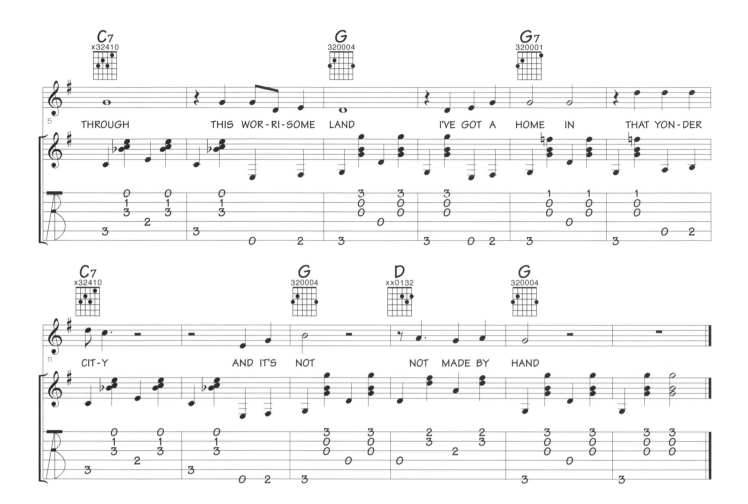

D BASS RUNS

How you play a bass run into a D chord depends on whether you're playing in the key of G or the key of D. Either way, you'll have to start on a fretted note, ending up on the open fourth string, which is the root of the D chord.

Let's do a bass run that works in the key of D. The notes of this run include another new note on the fretboard, a C♯ on the fifth string. C♯ is one fret, or a half step, above the C we've just been playing at the third fret, so you'll find C♯ at the fourth fret.

Example 5 shows the notes for the D bass run. In Example 6, the third note of the bass run, D, becomes the first bass note of a bass/strum pattern on D.

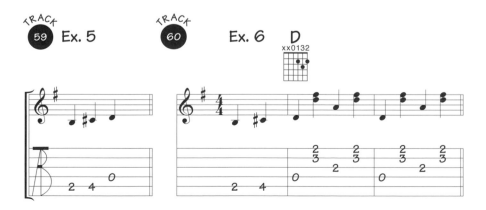

When you play a bass run into G or C, your ring finger is landing on the bottom note you need to fret for the chord you're about to play. It's almost as if the bass run is helping you get your fingers in place. Going into a D chord, playing the bass run doesn't help you get any of your fingers into the right place for the chord itself. However, the first note of a D-chord bass/strum pattern is the open D on the fourth string, so you have a whole beat free in which to get your fingers into place over on the top three strings. Also, as you finish the bass run, your index finger will have just been at the second fret of the fourth string, so it only has to come over one string, to the second fret of the third string, to be in place for the D chord.

In Example 7, practice staying on a D chord, dropping in the bass run every other time in place of the last bass/strum of the second measure. Then, in Example 8, try switching between a D and a G using a bass run into each chord.

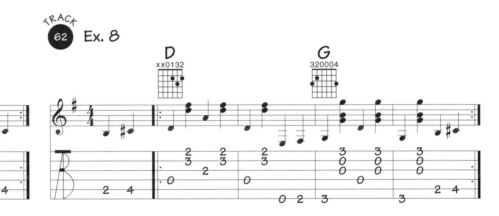

PLAY IT

"Bury Me beneath the Willow" is in the key of D, and we'll play it with bass runs into D and into G.

ESSENTIAL LISTENING

"Bury Me beneath the Willow," a particularly plaintive tale of unrequited love, has been recorded by many artists, past and present. Woody Guthrie plays it on *The Early Years* (Legacy); western swing bandleader Spade Cooley can be heard holding forth with a small group on *Radio Broadcasts 1945* (Country Routes). Modern flatpicker Tony Rice and mandolinist Ricky Skaggs included the tune on their duet record *Skaggs and Rice* (Sugar Hill), and for an instrumental version, investigate guitarist **Scott Nygaard**'s solo debut *No Hurry* (Rounder).

BURY ME BENEATH THE WILLOW

Verses 1, 2. See additional lyrics.

BUR - Y ME BE - NEATH THE WIL - LOW UN - DER THE

WEEP - ING WIL - LOW TREE WHEN SHE HEARS THAT

I AM SLEEP - ING MAY - BE THEN SHE'LL THINK OF ME

     D   G
BURY ME BENEATH THE WILLOW
     D   A
UNDER THE WEEPING WILLOW TREE
     D   G
WHEN SHE HEARS THAT I AM SLEEPING
     D   A   D
MAYBE THEN SHE'LL THINK OF ME

          D   G
1. SHE TOLD ME THAT SHE DID NOT LOVE ME
      D   A
   I COULDN'T BELIEVE THAT IT WAS TRUE
    D   G
   TILL I HEARD IT SOFTLY WHISPERED
    D   A   D
   SHE NO LONGER CARES FOR YOU

                  CHORUS

          D   G
2. ON MY GRAVE A SNOW WHITE LILY
       D   A
TO PROVE MY LOVE FOR HER WAS TRUE
     D   G
SHOW THE WORLD I DIED OF GRIEVING
     D   A   D
FOR THE LOVE I COULD NOT WIN

                  CHORUS

LESSON 9
BLUES BASICS

E7
020100

The blues is many things: a genre, a repertoire, a feel and a sensibility, and a form. As a genre, blues covers a dizzying variety of styles and artists; as a repertoire, it includes thousands of tunes both traditional and composed; the blues feeling and sensibility is a significant part of how musicians approach everything from jazz and rock to bluegrass and swing; and the 12-bar blues form is a cornerstone of all of those styles as well.

What do we mean by *form,* anyway? We've played fiddle tunes with an AABB form, where each A and each B section is eight bars long. There are many forms used in the blues repertoire, but the classic blues is 12 bars long and has the form AAB, where each section is four bars long. We've already encountered a version of the blues form in Lesson 2, with the tune "Stagolee." In the key of E, one of the simplest 12-bar blues has this chord progression:

TRACK 64 **Ex. 1**

12-Bar Blues Progression

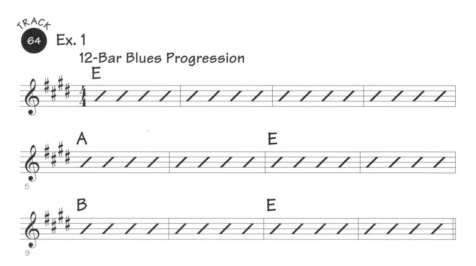

A7
x02030

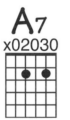

The AAB description comes as much from the arrangement of the lyrics as the chords, because the first line (A) is repeated before being answered in the B. And as you can see, there is actually some variation between the chords of the first and second A section.

One of the distinguishing sounds of the blues is the use of seventh chords for all three chords of the progression. We already know how to play a B7, so we'll need to add E7 and A7 to our chord stash. These are actually easy to learn, because for both of them, you just leave one note *out* of the regular chord.

To play an alternating bass/strum pattern on E7, remember to use the sixth string for the first bass note and the fifth string for the second bass note, just as you do on a regular E chord. And you can use the same alternating bass/strum pattern for A7 as you do for A.

TRACK
65 Ex. 2

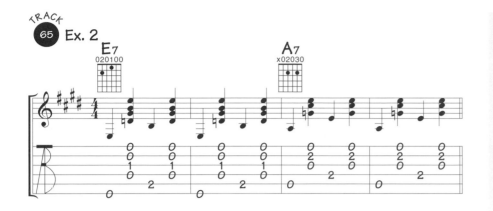

ESSENTIAL LISTENING

"Alberta" appears on any of a number of Leadbelly collections, including *My Last Go Round* (Recall) and *Complete Works,* Vol. 1 (Document). For two versions of a similar vintage, try Big Bill Broonzy's 1958 *Big Bill Broonzy Sings Folk Songs* (Smithsonian Folkways) or Snooks Eaglin's *New Orleans Street Singer* (Storyville). Geoff Muldaur's *The Secret Handshake* (HighTone) includes an excellent update of this tune, and Eric Clapton covered it on his *Unplugged* set (Warner Bros.).

BLUES RIFFS

Another characteristic of the blues is that sometimes a single blues phrase, or *riff,* will work with more than one chord. For example, start with the bass run in Example 3. The new note, G♯, is a half step (or one fret) above the G we know and love at the third fret of the sixth string. The natural sign (♮) next to the first note shows that this G is *not* sharp.

Now, we can use this bass run to kick off a bass/strum on an E7 chord, as in Example 4. We can use it to hang on an E7 chord for more than two bars, as in Example 5. We can use it to get from an E7 chord up to an A7 chord, as in Example 6, or to get from an A7 back down to E7, as in Example 7.

TRACK
66 Ex. 3

TRACK
67 Ex. 4

TRACK
68 Ex. 5

TRACK
69 Ex. 6

TRACK
70 Ex. 7

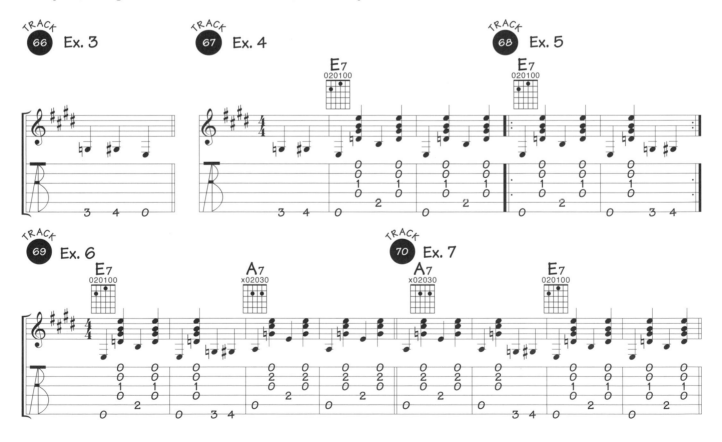

PLAY IT

Try out all these ideas in our next song, "Alberta," a 12-bar blues.

ALBERTA

	E	E7
1.	OH ALBERTA, WHERE'D YOU STAY LAST NIGHT?	
	A7	E
	OH ALBERTA, WHERE'D YOU STAY LAST NIGHT?	
	B7	E
	CAME HOME THIS MORNING, THE SUN WAS SHINING BRIGHT	

	E	E7
2.	IF YOU DON'T LOVE ME, WHY DON'T YOU TELL ME SO?	
	A7	E
	IF YOU DON'T LOVE ME, WHY DON'T YOU TELL ME SO?	
	B7	E
	I'M BROKENHEARTED, WITH NO PLACE TO GO	

	E	E7
3.	OH ALBERTA, WHERE YOU BEEN SO LONG?	
	A7	E
	OH ALBERTA, WHERE YOU BEEN SO LONG?	
	B7	E
	AIN'T HAD NO LOVIN' SINCE YOU'VE BEEN GONE	

LESSON 10
ALTERNATING-BASS FINGERPICKING

By now you may have noticed that picks are slippery things. No matter how many you start out with, you quickly lose all but one, which you then cling onto for weeks on end, wondering why you couldn't keep track of the previous half dozen the same way. Eventually they turn up in twos and threes at the bottom of the washing machine, where, presumably, they've been hanging out with all the single, unmatched socks. Who needs it?

So let's drop the pick again and add the alternating-bass sound into a finger-picking pattern. To keep things simple, we'll start with a picking pattern we already know, the one from Lesson 5. The bass notes that we use on the various chords won't be any different from what we've been playing in the last several songs, but now we'll be playing those bass notes with our thumb instead of a pick.

Here's how it works. On an E chord, our basic fingerpicking pattern goes like Example 1. When we do an alternating-bass/strum on an E chord now, we play Example 2. Combining the alternating bass from Example 2 with the picking pattern of Example 1, we get Example 3.

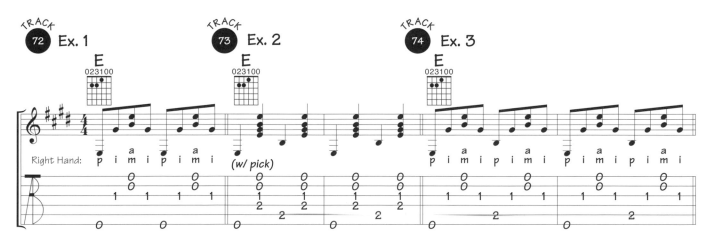

All we've basically done is borrow the upper bass note—the B at the second fret of the fifth string—and substituted it for the low E of the picking pattern, every other time. So now, instead of hitting E with our thumb every time, we hit E then B, E then B.

We can use the same idea on A, alternating the thumb between the fifth string and the fourth string as in Example 4. Once you can do that, your right hand doesn't change at all to play over a B7 chord; in Example 5, your thumb still alternates between the fifth string and the fourth string.

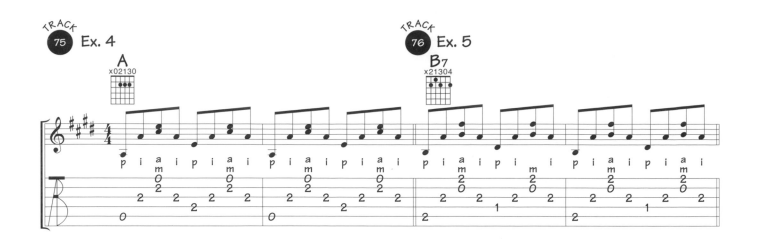

Now, practice these alternating-bass picking patterns over pairs of chords so that you can switch back and forth between E and A (Example 7) and between E and B7 (Example 8). Make sure you maintain the pattern in your right hand and hit the correct bass notes.

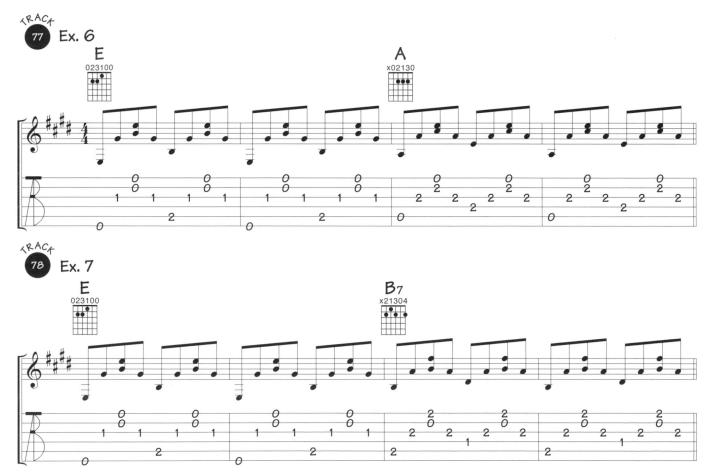

Now here's a tune to play with this alternating-bass picking pattern: "Sugar Babe."

SUGAR BABE

E

1. SUGAR BABE, I'M TIRED OF YOU
   A
   AIN'T YOUR LOVIN' BUT THE WAY YOU DO
   E   B7   E
   SUGAR BABE, IT'S ALL OVER NOW

E

2. ALL I WANT MY SUGAR TO DO
   A
   MAKE FIVE DOLLARS AND GIVE ME TWO
   E   B7   E
   SUGAR BABE, IT'S ALL OVER NOW

E

3. SUGAR BABE, WHAT'S THE MATTER WITH YOU
   A
   YOU DON'T TREAT ME LIKE YOU USED TO DO
   E   B7   E
   SUGAR BABE, IT'S ALL OVER NOW

E

4. SUGAR BABE, I'M TIRED OF YOU
   A
   AIN'T YOUR HONEY BUT THE WAY YOU DO
   E   B7   E
   SUGAR BABE, IT'S ALL OVER NOW

ESSENTIAL LISTENING

"Sugar Babe" is generally associated with Mance Lipscomb, a farmer and songster from Navasota, Texas, whose first name was short for "Emancipation." Listen to his performance on *Texas Songster* (Arhoolie); for an East Coast version, pick up Pink Anderson's *Ballad and Folk Singer*, Vol. 3 (Original Blues Classics). British folk guitarist John Renbourn's take can be heard on various reissues of his early work, including *John Renbourn/Another Monday* (Castle), and back in the States, check out old-time fiddler Bruce Molsky's *Bruce Molsky and Big Hoedown* (Rounder).

LESSON 11
FINGERPICKING IN 3/4

For our last lesson in Book 2, let's take a look at how our two main picking patterns can be adapted to play tunes in 3/4. We'll start with an E-minor chord and work our way up to the folk-blues classic "House of the Rising Sun."

The first pattern we learned, in Lesson 4, really lasts for only two beats if you just play it once: thumb, index, middle, ring. On an E-minor chord, that sounds like Example 1. To make it work in waltz time, or 3/4, we need to add one more beat. We can get that by coming back down the strings at the end, repeating the second and third strings with the middle and index fingers (Example 2). Try playing this pattern for a few measures in a row, as in Example 3.

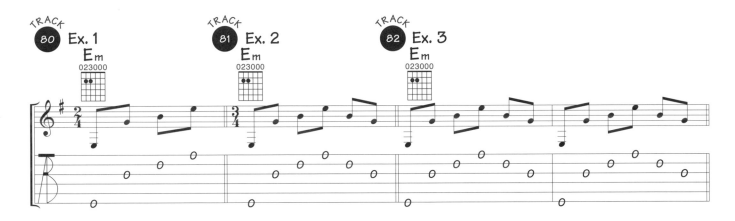

In Example 4, try it on a G chord. You can keep your picking hand on the same strings—sixth, third, second, and first. To play on an A-major chord (Example 5) or a C-major chord (Example 6), bring your thumb up to pick the fifth string, and keep your index, middle, and ring fingers on the top three strings. Example 7 shows this pattern on a B7 chord.

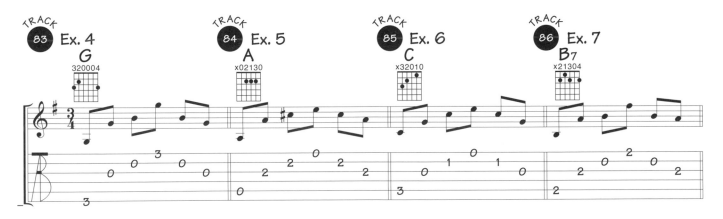

"HOUSE" RULES

"House of the Rising Sun" requires you to switch chords every bar, except in measures 7 and 8, when you hang on the B7 for two bars. In particular, we've never switched between A and C before, so you might want to isolate that change, as in Example 8:

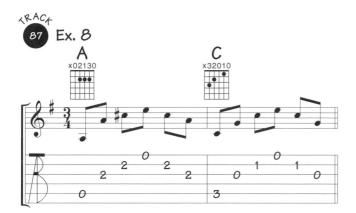

It's a good idea to practice making one-bar switches back and forth between each pair of chords: E minor to G and back, G to A and back, A to C and back, G to B7 and back, B7 to E minor and back.

On page 44 you'll find the entire tune. It has been recorded using a capo at the fifth fret, making this arrangement in the key of E minor *sound* in the key of A minor. You can play the song in E minor just the way it's written out, without the capo, if that's a good key for your voice. But if you want to sing in a higher key or practice along (many recorded versions of "House" are also in the key of A minor), place your capo at the fifth fret and keep everything else the same: play the exact same chords with the exact same picking pattern.

THE TONY RICE UNIT UNIT OF MEASURE

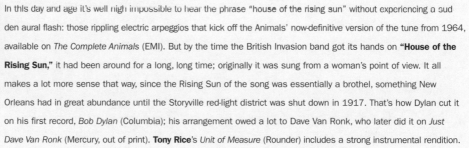

ESSENTIAL LISTENING

In this day and age it's well nigh impossible to hear the phrase "house of the rising sun" without experiencing a sudden aural flash: those rippling electric arpeggios that kick off the Animals' now-definitive version of the tune from 1964, available on *The Complete Animals* (EMI). But by the time the British Invasion band got its hands on **"House of the Rising Sun,"** it had been around for a long, long time; originally it was sung from a woman's point of view. It all makes a lot more sense that way, since the Rising Sun of the song was essentially a brothel, something New Orleans had in great abundance until the Storyville red-light district was shut down in 1917. That's how Dylan cut it on his first record, *Bob Dylan* (Columbia); his arrangement owed a lot to Dave Van Ronk, who later did it on *Just Dave Van Ronk* (Mercury, out of print). **Tony Rice**'s *Unit of Measure* (Rounder) includes a strong instrumental rendition.

HOUSE OF THE RISING SUN

```
        Em G     A         C                        Em    G    A      C
1.   THERE IS A HOUSE IN NEW ORLEANS           4.   GO TELL MY BABY SISTER
        Em     G      B7                              Em    G      B7
     THEY CALL THE RISING SUN                      NEVER DO LIKE I HAVE DONE
        Em      G      A        C                     Em     G      A     C
     AND IT'S BEEN THE RUIN OF MANY A POOR GIRL    BUT SHUN THAT HOUSE IN NEW ORLEANS
        Em    B7     Em    B7                         Em     B7    Em   B7
     AND ME, I KNOW I'M ONE                        THEY CALL THE RISING SUN


        Em    G    A      C                           Em      G     A         C
2.   MY MOTHER WAS A TAILOR                      5.   IT'S ONE FOOT ON THE PLATFORM
        Em      G        B7                             Em    G     B7
     SHE SEWED THESE NEW BLUE JEANS                 THE OTHER'S ON THE TRAIN
        Em     G    A       C                          Em   G    A      C
     MY SWEETHEART WAS A GAMBLER                    I'M GOING BACK TO NEW ORLEANS
     Em    B7      Em     B7                           Em      B7        Em    B7
     DOWN IN NEW ORLEANS                            TO WEAR THAT BALL AND CHAIN


        Em   G     A        C                         Em    G    A      C
3.   NOW THE ONLY THING A GAMBLER NEEDS          6.   I'M GOING BACK TO NEW ORLEANS
        Em    G     B7                                 Em    G     B7
     IS A SUITCASE AND A TRUNK                      MY RACE IS ALMOST RUN
        Em  G        A      C                          Em    G       A         C
     AND THE ONLY TIME HE'S SATISFIED              I'M GOING TO SPEND THE REST OF MY LIFE
     Em        B7     Em   B7                          Em     B7    Em   B7
     IS WHEN HE'S ON A DRUNK                        BENEATH THE RISING SUN
```

CONGRATULATIONS

You've made it through the second book of *The Acoustic Guitar Method*! We've covered a lot of ground—alternating-bass strums, bass runs, fingerpicking patterns, new chords, new scales, and of course, plenty of new tunes. As you may be realizing by now, each new chord, strum, or pattern you learn is both useful on its own and as a building block for what's coming next. Even as you play through these songs just for the enjoyment of it, you're solidifying your foundation, getting ready for what lies ahead in Book 3 and beyond. So take your time and let it all soak in. As you check out some of the recommended listening, feel free to start sorting out what you like best from the rest. And as always, no matter how wrapped up you get in it all, don't forget to pick up the guitar just because.

ABOUT THE AUTHOR

David Hamburger is a performer and writer who lives in Austin, Texas. He has been playing folk and blues music since first picking up the guitar at the age of 12 and has been on the faculty of the National Guitar Workshop since 1988. Hamburger's guitar, slide guitar, and Dobro playing can be heard on his solo albums *King of the Brooklyn Delta* (Chester, 1994) and *Indigo Rose* (Chester, 1999), as well as on numerous other independent recordings.

Hamburger is the author of four other books, including *Acoustic Guitar Slide Basics,* and has contributed dozens of lessons and articles to *Guitar Player* and *Acoustic Guitar* magazines. For a discography, performance schedule, and other information, visit his Web site at davidhamburger.com.

ACKNOWLEDGMENTS

Thanks to Jeffrey Pepper Rodgers for his detailed and patient editing; Andrew DuBrock for his equally careful attention to the music itself; David Lusterman for hatching this scheme in the first place; the Stringletter staff for all their various efforts, past, present, and future; Carl Thiel at Carl Thiel Music; Wayne Rooks; and Guadalupe Arts. Special thanks to Catherine Berry, who thinks that writing books is really cool. And to Lucille Magliozzi, wherever you are: all the things you taught me are in these pages somewhere.

ABOUT STRINGLETTER

Stringletter, which was founded in 1986, is the source for acoustic music magazines and books. We serve musicians, aficionados, and listeners with news, information, advice, and entertainment through a wide selection of products. Our specialty is music where songs and stringed instruments play a major role: roots, jazz, blues, rock, classical, and other traditional and contemporary styles. From songbooks to guide books to pictorial reference works, Stringletter books are enduring resources for acoustic musicians and students who want to improve their playing skills, expand their musical horizons, and become more knowledgeable about instruments and gear. Learn more at Stringletter.com.

Stringletter publishes *Acoustic Guitar,* the magazine for all acoustic guitar players, from beginners to performing professionals. Through interviews, reviews, workshops, sheet music, and song transcriptions, *Acoustic Guitar* readers learn music from around the globe and get to know the artists who create it. With product reviews and expert advice, *Acoustic Guitar* also helps readers become smarter buyers and owners of acoustic guitars and guitar gear. For more information, visit us on the web at AcousticGuitar.com.

Certificate of Completion

This certifies that

_____

has mastered *The Acoustic Guitar Method, Book Two.*

Teacher _____

Date _____

ACOUSTIC GUITAR

GUITAR LEARNING HAS GONE MOBILE

Acoustic Guitar U—The Next Level in Guitar Learning

No music book? No music stand? No sheet music? NO PROBLEM.

Log onto **AcousticGuitarU.com** from your PC, laptop, tablet, or smartphone and check out our ever-growing library of online guitar lessons, complete courses, and songs to learn. Enjoy:

- **Best-of-the-web audio and video instruction in a wide variety of styles and topics**

- **Easy-to-follow lessons for all levels from total beginner to advanced**

- **Streaming content, which means no more time spent waiting for files to download**

Learn acoustic guitar anytime, anywhere. All you need is access to the internet.